THE
SIBERIAN HUSKY

by Charlotte Wilcox

Content reviewed by:
The Siberian Husky Club of
the Twin Cities, Inc.

CAPSTONE
HIGH-INTEREST
BOOKS

an imprint of Capstone Press
Mankato, Minnesota

Capstone High-Interest Books are published by Capstone Press
151 Good Counsel Drive, P.O. Box 669, Mankato, Minnesota 56002
http://www.capstone-press.com

Library of Congress Cataloging-in-Publication Data
Wilcox, Charlotte.
    The Siberian husky/by Charlotte Wilcox.
       p. cm. — (Learning about dogs)
    Includes bibliographical references (p. 45) and index.
    Summary: Describes this dog of the far North including its physical
characteristics, its use for pulling sleds, the development of the breed, its value
as a companion, and its required needs.
    ISBN 0-7368-0007-7
    1. Siberian huskies—Juvenile literature. [1. Siberian huskies. 2. Dogs.]
I. Title. II. Series: Wilcox, Charlotte. Learning about dogs.
SF429.S65W55 1999
636.73—dc21
                                                                  98-3564
                                                                     CIP
                                                                      AC

Editorial Credits
Matt Doeden, editor; Timothy Halldin, cover designer and illustrator;
    Sheri Gosewisch, photo researcher
Photo Credits
Kent & Donna Dannen, 4, 9, 12, 38
Mark Raycroft, 6, 14, 25, 29, 32, 35
Photo Network/Henry T. Kaiser, cover
Unicorn Stock Photos/Betts Anderson, 36; H.H. Thomas, 40
The University of Alaska Fairbanks, 17, 18, 23
Visuals Unlimited/Steve McCutcheon, 10, 26; Mark E. Gibson, 30

2 3 4 5 6 05 04 03 02

Table of Contents

Quick Facts about the Siberian Husky

Description

Height:

Male Siberian Huskies stand 21 to 23 and one-half inches (53 to 60 centimeters) tall. Females stand 20 to 22 inches (51 to 56 centimeters) tall. Height is measured from the ground to the withers. The withers are the tops of the shoulders.

Weight:

Males weigh from 45 to 60 pounds (20 to 27 kilograms). Females weigh from 35 to 50 pounds (16 to 23 kilograms).

Physical features:	Many people think Siberian Huskies look like wolves. But Siberians are much smaller and have different markings. Many have brown or blue eyes. Some have one eye of each color. Some have two colors in one or both eyes.
Colors:	Siberian Huskies can be white and black, white and red, or white and gray. Some are all white or all black. Most have all white faces or white faces with dark markings called a mask.

Development

Place of origin:	The first Siberian Huskies came from an area of Russia called Siberia.
History of breed:	Siberian Huskies came from Asian sled dogs hundreds of years ago.
Numbers:	The American Kennel Club registers about 10,000 Siberian Huskies each year. Register means to record a dog's breeding record with an official club. The Canadian Kennel Club registers about 2,000 Siberian Huskies each year.

Uses

Siberian Huskies pull sleds in races. Many are kept as pets.

Chapter 1
Dogs of the North

Dogs are important to people who live in the far North. This area includes the northern parts of Europe, Asia, North America, and also the Arctic. Northern people use dogs for many jobs. Some dogs hunt. Others guard or herd livestock. Siberian Huskies' main job is to pull sleds.

Siberians are Northern dogs. Northern dogs share common features. They have long muzzles, pointed ears, and bushy tails. A muzzle is a dog's nose, mouth, and jaw. Their layers of thick fur help them stay warm in cold temperatures.

Northern dogs have long muzzles and pointed ears.

Sled Dogs

Northern people have used sled dogs for at least 3,000 years. Years ago, people had few ways to travel in cold climates. They taught dogs to pull sleds. Dogs pulled supplies on sleds over miles of snowy ground.

Different types of dogs learned to pull sleds. Large dogs such as Alaskan Malamutes pull heavy loads. Large dogs usually are slower than small dogs. Smaller dogs such as Siberian Huskies are fast. They can pull lighter loads over long distances.

Siberians are popular sled dogs. They can pull one and one-half times their own weight. Siberians also make good pets. People often call them Siberians for short.

Siberian Huskies are among the fastest sled dogs.

Chapter 2

The Beginnings of the Breed

North Americans brought Siberian Huskies to Alaska from northeastern Asia. The Chukchi people from the Russian region of Siberia used the dogs for transportation. They used Siberians to carry people and supplies on sleds. The Chukchi people were also hunters. They sometimes used Siberians to pull large whales onto the ice while hunting.

Early Sled-dog Races

During the early 1900s, dogsleds provided a major means of transportation in Alaska. Most people used large dogs such as Alaskan

Dogsleds once provided a major means of transportation in Alaska.

Each sled dog wears a harness.

Malamutes as sled dogs. People bragged about their sled dogs. They held contests to see who had the best sled dogs. This was the beginning of the sled-dog racing sport.

Sled-dog teams varied in size. They could have as few as two dogs. Some teams had more than 20 dogs. Each dog wore a harness around its body. The dogs' harnesses were connected by a set of straps called a gangline.

The gangline connected the dogs to a cart or sled. Drivers controlled the dogs by voice. The French command for "go" sounded like "mush." People called dogsled drivers mushers because of this command.

In 1908, people in Nome, Alaska, staged a public race. They called it the All Alaska Sweepstakes. The race covered 408 miles (657 kilometers) from Nome to Candle, Alaska, and back. None of the racers used Siberian Huskies to pull their sleds.

The All Alaska Sweepstakes was a huge success. People began looking for dogs to enter in the 1909 race.

William Goosak

William Goosak was a fur trader. He wanted to find sled dogs that were faster than Alaskan Malamutes. He went to Siberia to find new dogs. He bought dogs from the Chukchi people. These dogs were early Siberian Huskies.

Goosak brought these dogs back to Nome. They were smaller than most sled dogs of that time. People did not think much of Goosak's

dogs. They called the dogs Siberian rats.

Goosak entered a team of Siberians in the 1909 All Alaska Sweepstakes. He hired Louis Thrustrup to drive his dogsled. Thrustrup was known as a skilled musher. But few people believed the Siberians could compete with larger Alaskan Malamutes.

The 1909 All Alaska Sweepstakes

There was a huge storm the day the 1909 Sweepstakes began. Blowing snow blinded mushers and buried the trail. Most of the sled-dog teams gave up. Only three teams kept going. Two were teams of Alaskan dogs. These dogs knew the trail well.

Thrustrup's team also stayed in the race. His dogs had never been on the trail before. But somehow they stayed on course through the storm. The Alaskan teams stopped to rest when they finally reached Candle. But Thrustrup's team did not rest. Thrustrup's team turned around right away and headed back to Nome.

Few people believed small Siberian Huskies could compete with large Alaskan Malamutes.

Thrustrup's dogs grew tired before they reached Nome. Thrustrup let the dogs rest by carrying one dog at a time on his sled. The team could not keep up its speed. Both Alaskan teams finished the race in about 82 hours. Thrustrup's team finished in 89 hours. But people were impressed by Thrustrup's Siberians.

The 1910 Sweepstakes

People wanted to learn more about Siberian Huskies after the 1909 Sweepstakes. One musher named Fox Maule Ramsay went to Siberia and bought about 60 Siberians.

Ramsay wanted to win the 1910 Sweepstakes. He picked his 12 best Siberians for his sled-dog team. He hired another musher to drive a second team. He placed 12 more of his dogs on that team.

Ramsay had one good lead dog left. The lead dog guides the team and sets the sled's speed. The dog's name was Kolyma. Ramsay hired a third musher named John Johnson to

John Johnson's team of Siberian Huskies won the 1910 All Alaska Sweepstakes.

drive a third dogsled. Ramsay picked the remaining dogs for the team. But Ramsay did not think Johnson's team of dogs was good enough to win.

Johnson's team won the 1910 Sweepstakes. Johnson's team finished the race in 74 hours. No team ever beat that record.

Chapter 3

The Development of the Breed

Roald Amundsen came to Nome in 1914. He was a famous explorer from Norway. Amundsen was planning a trip to the North Pole. He needed dogs for his trip.

A musher named Leonhard Seppala helped Amundsen pick a team of Siberian Huskies for the trip. Seppala chose the best Siberians in Alaska at that time. Seppala believed the team could make the trip to the North Pole.

Amundsen later decided not to go to the North Pole. Seppala kept Amundsen's dogs as a sled-dog team. Seppala's team won the All

Leonhard Seppala and his team of Siberian Huskies won the All Alaska Sweepstakes in 1915, 1916, and 1917.

The Great Serum Run

Alaska Sweepstakes in 1915, 1916, and 1917. Seppala used the dogs in this team to breed more Siberians.

The Great Serum Run

In January 1925, many people in Nome became sick with diphtheria. Diphtheria is a deadly illness. People in Nome needed serum to cure the diphtheria. Serum is a medicine that helps fight off illnesses. There was not enough serum in Nome to treat everyone. Many lives were in danger.

The nearest supply of serum was about 1,000 miles (1,609 kilometers) away in Anchorage, Alaska. A train carried the serum to Nenana, Alaska. But the railroad tracks ended there. Nenana was still 674 miles (1,085 kilometers) from Nome.

The only way to get the serum to Nome was by dogsled. The Iditarod Trail went from Anchorage to Nome. Most sled-dog teams needed two to three weeks to travel from Nenana to Nome. But people in Nome needed the serum sooner. Mushers from across Alaska decided to work together to complete the trip as quickly as possible.

A musher named Bill Shannon began the trip with the serum. Shannon left Nenana at 9 p.m. on January 27. He took the serum 53 miles (85 kilometers). Then he handed it to another musher. About 20 different dogsled teams carried the serum during the journey.

Seppala's Dogs

Seppala's team traveled the longest part of the serum run. Seppala's lead dog was one of the most famous Siberian Huskies ever. The dog's name was Togo. Seppala's team traveled 172 miles (277 kilometers) to get the serum. It then carried the serum 96 miles (155 kilometers). They made the entire trip in less than 12 hours.

Gunnar Kaasen was the last musher to carry the serum. He drove a team of Seppala's Siberians. A dark-colored Siberian named Balto was Kaasen's lead dog.

Kaasen's team brought the serum into Nome. The team reached Nome at 5:30 a.m. on

Togo led Seppala's team on the Great Serum Run.

February 2. The trip from Nenana to Nome took one week. The serum saved many lives.

Balto and Togo

The serum-run mushers were heroes. Newspapers across the United States and Canada printed stories about the trip. People wanted to see the dogs. Kaasen took Balto's team to California. They were the first sled dogs most people there had seen.

Seppala took Togo and about 40 other dogs to New England in the northeastern United States. Sled-dog racing was popular there during the 1920s. Seppala let a musher named Elizabeth Nansen drive his team of dogs in a New England race. Nansen's team won the race.

Seppala gave Togo to Nansen. Nansen started breeding Siberians in New England. Later, Seppala brought more Siberian Huskies to New England and the Canadian province of Quebec. Most modern Siberians came from Seppala's dogs.

Most modern Siberian Huskies came from Seppala's dogs.

Chapter 4

The Siberian Husky Today

Today, people rely less on sled dogs for travel. Other forms of transportation have replaced dogsleds throughout much of the North.

Sled-dog races are still popular in the North. The Iditarod Trail Sled Dog Race begins each year in Anchorage. The race follows the old Iditarod Trail to Nome. The Iditarod is the longest sled-dog race in the world. It covers more than 1,150 miles (1,850 kilometers). It lasts between 10 and 15 days.

Sled-dog races are still popular in the North.

The Yukon Quest is a 1,000-mile (1,609-kilometer) sled-dog race. The race crosses the Yukon Territory in Canada.

Appearance

Siberian Huskies are medium-size dogs. They are lean and strong. Males stand 21 to 23 and one-half inches (53 to 60 centimeters) tall. Females stand 20 to 22 inches (51 to 56 centimeters) tall. Males weigh 45 to 60 pounds (20 to 27 kilograms). Females weigh 35 to 50 pounds (16 to 23 kilograms).

Siberians have two layers of thick fur. The outer layer is rough and straight. This is called guard hair. The inner layer is soft and warm. This is called the undercoat.

Siberians can be many colors. Most are white and black, white and red, or white and gray. Most have all white faces or white faces with dark markings called a mask.

Siberian Huskies have thick fur.

Siberians have brown or blue eyes. Some
have one eye of each color. Some have two
colors in one or both eyes. Siberians have
long muzzles. The muzzles can be black,
brown, or pink.

Grizzly

Siberian Huskies are friendly dogs. They can
also be brave. One Michigan musher learned
just how brave Siberians can be when his
team saved his life.

The musher was driving his team of
Siberians through the woods. Grizzly was
the lead dog of his team. A bear attacked
the musher.

Grizzly turned the team of dogs toward the
bear while the owner tried to escape. Grizzly
charged the bear while still in his harness.
This gave the man time to climb a tree.
Grizzly and the other dogs stayed under the
tree for seven hours. They were still there
when searchers arrived.

**Siberian Huskies have long muzzles. Their noses are
black, brown, or pink.**

Chapter 5

Owning a Siberian Husky

Siberian Huskies are playful pets. They get along well with children and other dogs. Siberians need more exercise than some other breeds do. Owners must be sure their Siberians have plenty of time outdoors.

Keeping a Siberian Husky
Siberian Huskies can be house dogs. They seem to enjoy the company of people. But owners who keep Siberians indoors must exercise their dogs regularly on a leash or in a fenced yard.

Siberian Huskies need to exercise outdoors. But they should never be allowed to run loose.

Owners must make sure their dogs stay cool during summer. They should make sure their dogs have plenty of shade and water during warm weather. Too much heat could stress or kill any dog.

Owners should never let their Siberians run free. Siberians are independent dogs. They may not come home if they are free. Owners should make sure their Siberians have identification tags in case the dogs leave their homes.

Siberians rarely bark, but sometimes they howl. Owners must make sure their dogs do not bother neighbors with their howling.

Feeding a Siberian

Siberian Huskies do not need much food. They eat less than other dogs their size. But they need more fat and protein than other dogs. Meat and fish are good sources of fat and protein. Most owners feed Siberians dry

Siberian Huskies sometimes howl.

dog food. They add meat, fish, or oil for extra fat and protein.

Each Siberian eats a different amount. The amount Siberians eat depends on the amount of exercise they get and their age.

Siberians need plenty of water all the time. It is especially important that owners give their dogs enough water during warm weather.

Finding a Siberian

People who want Siberian Husky puppies should contact a local Siberian club. These clubs help people find responsible breeders. Clubs also organize sled-dog races and other events.

Good breeders do not sell Siberians through pet stores. Most breeders warn people not to buy dogs at pet stores. These dogs often are unhealthy. They may not be used to people.

Some people buy Siberians from rescue shelters. Rescue shelters find homes for abandoned dogs. Dogs from rescue shelters

The amount Siberian Huskies eat depends on the amount of exercise they get and their age.

usually cost less than breeders' dogs. Some are even free. Many rescued dogs already are trained.

Enjoying a Siberian Husky

Siberian Huskies have a natural ability to pull sleds. Even people who keep just one or two Siberians can enjoy racing activities with their dogs. One or two Siberians can pull a small sled. They learn commands easily.

Siberians are good at skijoring. Skijoring is a sport in which one or two dogs pull a person on skies. This can be a healthy and fun activity for owners and their dogs.

Siberian Huskies have a natural ability to pull sleds.

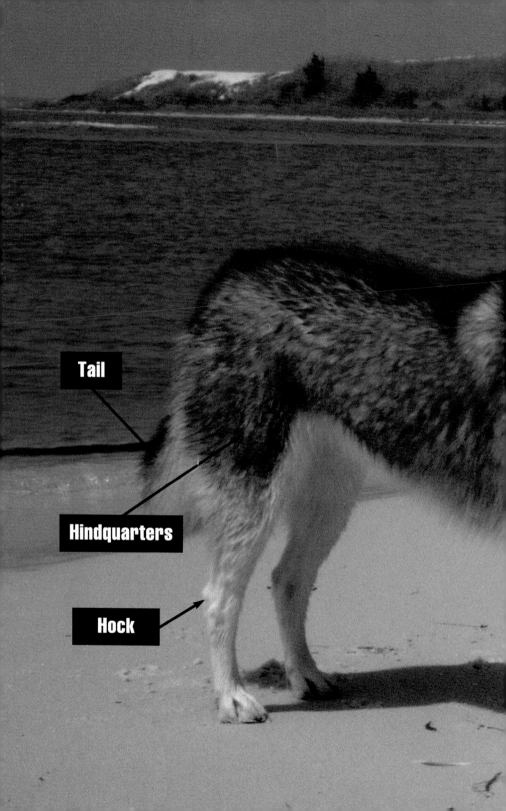

Tail

Hindquarters

Hock

Quick Facts about Dogs

Dog Terms

A male dog is called a dog. A female dog is called a bitch. A young dog is a puppy until it is one year old. A newborn puppy is a whelp until it no longer depends on its mother's milk. A family of puppies born at one time is called a litter.

Life History

Origin: All dogs, wolves, coyotes, and dingoes descended from a single wolflike species. Dogs have been friends of people since early times.

Types: There are about 350 different dog breeds. Dogs come in different sizes and colors. Adult dogs weigh from two to 200 pounds (one to 91 kilograms). They stand from six to 36 inches (15 to 91 centimeters) tall.

Reproduction: Dogs mature at six to 18 months. Puppies are born two months after breeding. An average litter is three to six puppies, but litters of 15 or more are possible.

Development: Newborn puppies cannot see or hear. Their ears and eyes open one to two weeks after birth. They try to walk about two weeks after birth. Their teeth begin to come in about three weeks after birth.

Life span: Dogs are fully grown at two years. They may live up to 15 years.

The Dog's Super Senses

Smell: Dogs have a strong sense of smell. Dogs use their noses even more than their eyes and ears. They recognize people, animals, and objects just by smelling them. They may recognize smells from long distances. They also may remember smells for long periods of time.

Hearing: Dogs hear better than people do. Dogs can hear noises from long distances. They also hear high-pitched sounds that people cannot hear.

Sight: Dogs' eyes are on the sides of their heads. They can see twice as wide around their heads as people can. Some scientists believe dogs cannot see colors.

Touch: Dogs enjoy being petted more than almost any other animal. They also can feel vibrations from approaching trains or the earliest stages of earthquakes.

Taste: Dogs cannot taste much. This is partly because their sense of smell is so strong that it overpowers their taste.

Navigation: Dogs often can find their way through crowded streets or across miles of wilderness without any guidance. This is a special ability that scientists do not fully understand.

Words to Know

diphtheria (dif-THIHR-ee-uh)—a deadly illness

gangline (GANG-line)—a set of straps that connects a team of sled dogs to a cart or sled

register (REJ-uh-stur)—to record a dog's breeding records with an official club

serum (SIHR-uhm)—a liquid that helps fight off illnesses

Siberia (sye-BIHR-ee-uh)—an area of land in northeastern Asia

skijoring (skee-JOR-ing)—a sport in which one or two dogs pull a person on skis

transportation (transs-pur-TAY-shuhn)—the system and means of moving people and supplies

withers (WITH-urs)—the tops of an animal's shoulders

To Learn More

Crisman, Ruth. *Racing the Iditarod Trail.* New York: Dillon Press, 1993.

Paulsen, Gary. *Puppies, Dogs, and Blue Northers.* San Diego: Harcourt Brace and Company, 1996.

Ring, Elizabeth. *Sled Dogs: Arctic Athletes.* Good Dogs! Brookfield, Conn.: Millbrook Press, 1994.

Shahan, Sherry. *Dashing through the Snow: The Story of the Jr. Iditarod.* Brookfield, Conn.: Millbrook Press, 1997.

You can read articles about Siberian Huskies in magazines such as *AKC Gazette, Dog Fancy, Dogs in Canada, Dog World, Team and Trail, Mushing,* and *The Siberian Quarterly.*

Useful Addresses

American Kennel Club
5580 Centerview Drive, Suite 200
Raleigh, NC 27606

Canadian Kennel Club
89 Skyway Avenue, Suite 100
Etobicoke, ON M9W 6R4
Canada

International Siberian Husky Club
North 7002 Peek Station Road
Elkhorn, WI 53121-9417

Siberian Husky Club of America
210 Madera Drive
Victoria, TX 77905-0611

Siberian Husky Club of Canada
R.R. 1
Selkirk, ON N0A 1P0
Canada

Internet Sites

Alaska Dog Musher Association
http://www.sleddog.org

Iditarod
http://www.iditarod.com

International Sled Dog Racing Association
http://www.uslink.net/~isdra

John Beargrease Sled Dog Marathon
http://www.beargrease.com

Siberian Husky Club of America
http://www.shca.org

Index